RHYTHMS

Volume Two

by
Bruce Arnold

Muse Eek Publishing Company
New York, New York

ISBN 1-890944-56-4

Printed in the United States

This publication can be purchased from your local bookstore, on-line via our shopping cart, or by contacting:
Muse Eek Publishing Company
P.O. Box 509
New York, NY 10276, USA
Toll Free in USA: 866-415-8960
Phone: 212-473-7030
Fax: 212-473-4601
http://www.muse-eek.com
sales@muse-eek.com

Table Of Contents

Acknowledgments

The author would like to thank Michal Shapiro for proof reading and helpful suggestions. I would also like to thank my students who through their questions helped me to see their needs so that I might address them as best I could.

About the Author

Bruce Arnold is from Sioux Falls, South Dakota. His educational background started with 3 years of music study at the University of South Dakota; he then attended the Berklee College of Music where he received a Bachelor of Music degree in composition. During that time he also studied privately with Jerry Bergonzi and Charlie Banacos.

Mr. Arnold has taught at some of the most prestigious music schools in America, including the New England Conservatory of Music, Dartmouth College, Berklee College of Music, Princeton University and New York University. He is a performer, composer, jazz clinician and has an extensive private instruction practice.

Currently Mr. Arnold is performing with his own "The Bruce Arnold Trio," and "Eye Contact" with Harvie Swartz, as well as with two experimental bands, "Release the Hounds" a free improv group, and "Spooky Actions" which re-interprets the work of 20th Century classical masters.

His debut CD "Blue Eleven" (MMC 2036J) received great critical acclaim, and his most recent CD "A Few Dozen" was released in January 2000. The Los Angeles Times said of this release "Mr. Arnold deserves credit for his effort to expand the jazz palette."

For more information about Mr. Arnold check his website at http://www.arnoldjazz.com This website contains audio examples of Mr. Arnold's compositions and a workshop section with free downloadable music exercises.

Foreword

Many of my students have asked me how they can improve their comprehension and execution of rhythms. This book is an attempt to fill those needs.

Although there are many books out that help you learn your rhythms this series of books is unique in that each example is accompanied by an audio example. These audio examples can be downloaded for free from the internet at http://www.muse-eek.com. The audio files use midifiles which can be played on a Mac or IBM computer by using a midifileplayer or any sequencer program. Midifile players are available for free at many sites on the internet. muse-eek.com lists a few places to download this software.

This book is part of a sight reading series aimed at getting a student proficient at recognizing and playing rhythms. Other volumes in this series will introduce melodic shapes in different stylistic contexts. See the final pages of this book for a complete listing and description of current music related publications.

Muse Eek Publishing has created a website with a FAQ forum for all my books. If you have any questions about anything contained in this book feel free to contact me at FAQ@muse-eek.com and I will happy to post an answer to your question. My goal is to educate and help you reach a higher degree of musical ability.

Bruce Arnold
New York, New York

How to use this book

This book can be used to learn sight reading and to learn rhythms. There are some definite right and wrong ways to approach this goal. If you are a total beginner, obviously you will have to first learn the subdivisions of a measure and what each eighth note or sixteenth note rhythm sounds like. This may require you to subdivide a measure or a beat in your head. For instance, the eighth note rhythm in Example 1 could be subdivided by counting eighth notes in your head as you play the rhythm.

Example 1

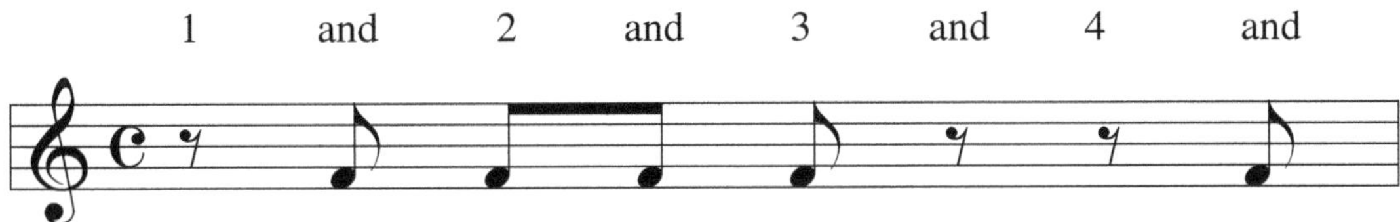

Example 2 shows how you might subdivide a sixteenth note measure. Though this type of subdividing may help initially to figure out a rhythm, in the long run is a very bad idea to develop a habit like this. It is much better not to count at all, but to "feel" the rhythm. This "feeling" requires that you know what the rhythm sounds like before you play it. This instant recognition of a written rhythm can be developed by trusting your internal rhythmic clock, relaxing, and memorizing the sounds of all rhythms. This may seem like a daunting task considering how many rhythmic combinations there are but look at this as a long range project. You will be reading music for the rest of your life, so start now.

Example 2

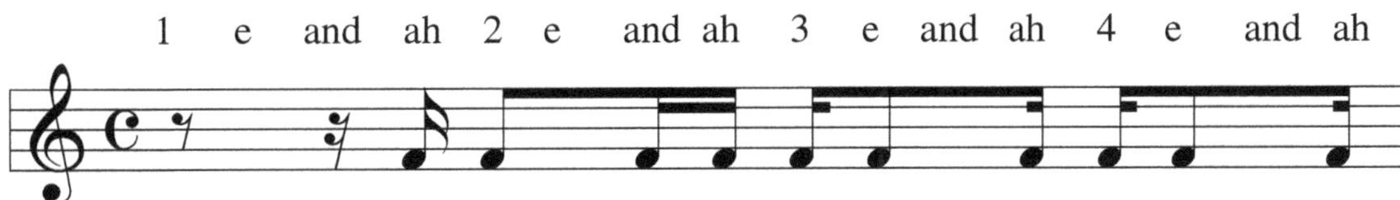

To tap or not to tap (your foot) that is the question. It is much better to get out of the habit of tapping your foot. Too many students start off relying on their foot to keep them in time rather than their internal musical sense. Trust yourself and over time your feel, time and accuracy will improve. It is one thing to tap your foot as a response to playing music, it is another to be tapping your foot to keep time. "Feeling" rhythms will give you better time and make your reading more musical.

On any instrument economy of motion is important especially as the tempo increases. With all exercises found in this book make sure to move your hands and fingers as little as possible while at the same time keeping them relaxed. If you are a guitar player I would recommend my Right Hand Technique Book ISBN 0-9648632-6-X as a companion book to help you develop the proper right hand technique.

You should also read the examples found in this book with both a straight eighth or a "swing" feel. The audio examples found on my website have the straight eighth feel. To work on using a swing feel I recommend getting together with a drummer or playing along with your favorite swing drummer on CD. Most swing tunes are written out using the rhythmic level found in book one of this series i.e. eighth notes. Contemporary fusion compositions that incorporate Rap and Hip Hop grooves use the sixteenth note metric level found in this book. Therefore it is a good idea to read these rhythms with a swing feel.

Over my many years of reading I have found that manuscript and notation methods make a big difference on how the eye reacts when sight reading. In order to get your eye used to reading many types of manuscripts, go to your local library and check out any music you can find and read it. You will find that what I'm saying is true. Some manuscripts will be easy, while others will take time before your eye adjusts. Also try to find as much hand written music as possible. This will prepare you for those people you run into whose written notation is close to illegible.

The notation method used in Volume One and Volume Two of this series is the notation commonly found in jazz and rock circles and is usually referred to as traditional notation. This form of notation has one important feature, the "imaginary bar line" which is used so the reader can always divide a measure in half visually. (see example 4) It is a lot easier to recognize what is going on rhythmically and melodically in half a measure than in a whole measure.

1. If you look at example 3 you will see that it is difficult to see where the 3rd beat of the measure begins. In example 4 an imaginary bar line has been added making the beginning of the 3rd beat clear.

Example 3 (Modern Notation)

Example 4 (Traditional Notation)

For a seasoned sight reader the imaginary bar line becomes cumbersome. Common rhythm patterns as shown in example 5 are replaced by the modern notation shown in example 6.

Example 5 shows traditional notation.

Example 6 shows modern notation.

Modern notation allows the composer and the experienced sight reader a short hand notation method that is quick to write and recognize. Further volumes of this rhythm series will cover modern notation. If you read a lot of classical music I'm sure you have come across many of these modern notation examples.

EXERCISE 1

17
19
3
21
3
23
3
3
3
25
3
27
3
29
3
3
31
3
3
33
3
3

35
37
39
41
43
45
47
49
51

53
3
3
55
3
3
57
3
3
59
61
63
3
3
3
65
67
3
69
3

71
73
75
77
79
81
83
85
87

89
91
3
3
93
3
3
95
97
3
99
3
101
3
103
3
3
105
3
3
3
3
3
3
3

107
109
3
3
111
113
115
117
3
119
121
123

125
127
129
131
133
135
137
139
141

143
3
3
3
3
3
3
145
147
3
3
149
3

EXERCISE 2

17
19
21
23
25
3
3
3
27
3
29
31
33

35
3
3
37
3
3
39
41
3
43
3
3
45
3
47
3
3
49
51

53
3
3
55
57
59
3
3
61
3
3
63
3
65
3
3
3
3
67
69
3
3

71
73
75
3
3
3
3
77
3
79
81
83
85
3
87
3
3

89
91
93
95
97
3
3
99
3
101
103
3
3
3
105

107
109
111
113
115
117
119
121
123
3
3
3

125
3
3
127
129
3
131
133
3
3
135
3
3
137
139
3
3
3
141

143
3
3
145
3
147
3
3
149
3
3

EXERCISE 3

17
19
21
3
3
23
25
3
27
3
29
31
33
3
3
35

37
3
3
39
3
41
3
43
3
45
47
49
51
53
55

57
3
3
59
3
3
61
3
3
63
3
65
67
3
3
3
3
69
3
3
71
3
73
3
3
3
75

77
79
81
83
85
87
89
91
93
95

97
99
101
3
103
3
3
3
105
3
107
109
3
3
111
3
3
113
115
3
3

117
3
119
121
3
3
123
3
3
125
127
129
131
133
3
135

137
139
141
3
3
143
145
147
3
3
3
3
149
151
153
3
3
3
155

157
159
161
3
163
165
3
3

EXERCISE 4

19
21
3
3
3
3
3
3
23
25
27
3
3
29
31
33
35
3
3
3
37

39
3
41
43
45
3
3
3
3
47
3
49
3
3
51
53
55
3
3
3
57

59
61
3
63
65
3
3
67
69
71
73
3
75
3
77

79
3
3
81
83
85
3
3
87
89
91
93
3
95
3
3
3
97

99
101
103
105
107
109
111
113
115
117

119
121
123
3
125
3
127
129
131
133
3
135
3
3
137

139
3
3
141
3
3
143
145
3
3
147
149
151
153
3
3
155
157

159
3
3
3
161
163
3
3
165

EXERCISE 5

17
19
21
23
25
27
29
31
33
35

37
3
39
3
3
41
3
43
45
3
3
3
47
3
3
49
3
3
3
3
51
3
53
55
3
3

57
3
3
59
3
3
61
63
65
67
3
69
71
73
75

77
79
81
83
85
3
3
87
89
91
93
95
3

97
3
3
3
99
3
3
101
103
3
105
3
107
3
109
3
3
111
3
3
3
113
115

117
119
121
123
125
127
129
131
133
135

137
3
3
139
141
3
3
3
3
143
3
3
145
3
3
3
147
3
3
149
3
151
3
3
153
155

157
159
3
161
163

EXERCISE 6

17
3
3
19
3
3
21
3
3
23
25
3
27
29
31
33
3
3
3

35
37
3
3
3
39
3
3
3
41
43
3
3
3
45
47
3
3
49
51

53
3
55
3
3
57
59
3
61
63
3
3
3
3
65
3
3
67
3
3
69

71
3
73
75
3
77
79
3
3
81
3
83
3
3
85
87
3
3
3

89
3
3
91
3
93
95
97
3
3
99
101
103
105
3

107
3
109
3
3
3
111
113
115
117
119
3
3
3
121
123

125
3
127
129
131
133
135
3
3
3
137
139
3
3
141
3
3

143
145
3
3
147
149
3
3

EXERCISE 7

17
19
21
23
25
27
29
31
33

35
3
37
39
41
3
3
43
45
47
49
3
51
3

53
55
57
59
61
3
63
65
3
3
3
67
3
3
69

71
3
3
3
3
3
73
3
3
75
3
3
77
3
79
81
83
3
3
85
3
87

89
91
3
93
3
3
95
97
99
3
101
103
105
3

107
3
3
109
111
3
3
113
115
117
119
3
3
121
3
123
3

125
3
3
127
129
3
3
3
131
3
3
133
135
3
3
137
139
3
141
3
3

143
145
3
3
147
149
3
3

EXERCISE 8

17
19
3
21
23
25
3
3
27
3
29
3
3
3
3
31
33
3
3

53
55
57
59
61
3
3
3
63
65
3
67
69
3

71
3
73
75
77
3
79
3
81
83
85
87
3
3
3
3

89
91
3
3
93
95
97
3
99
3
101
103
105

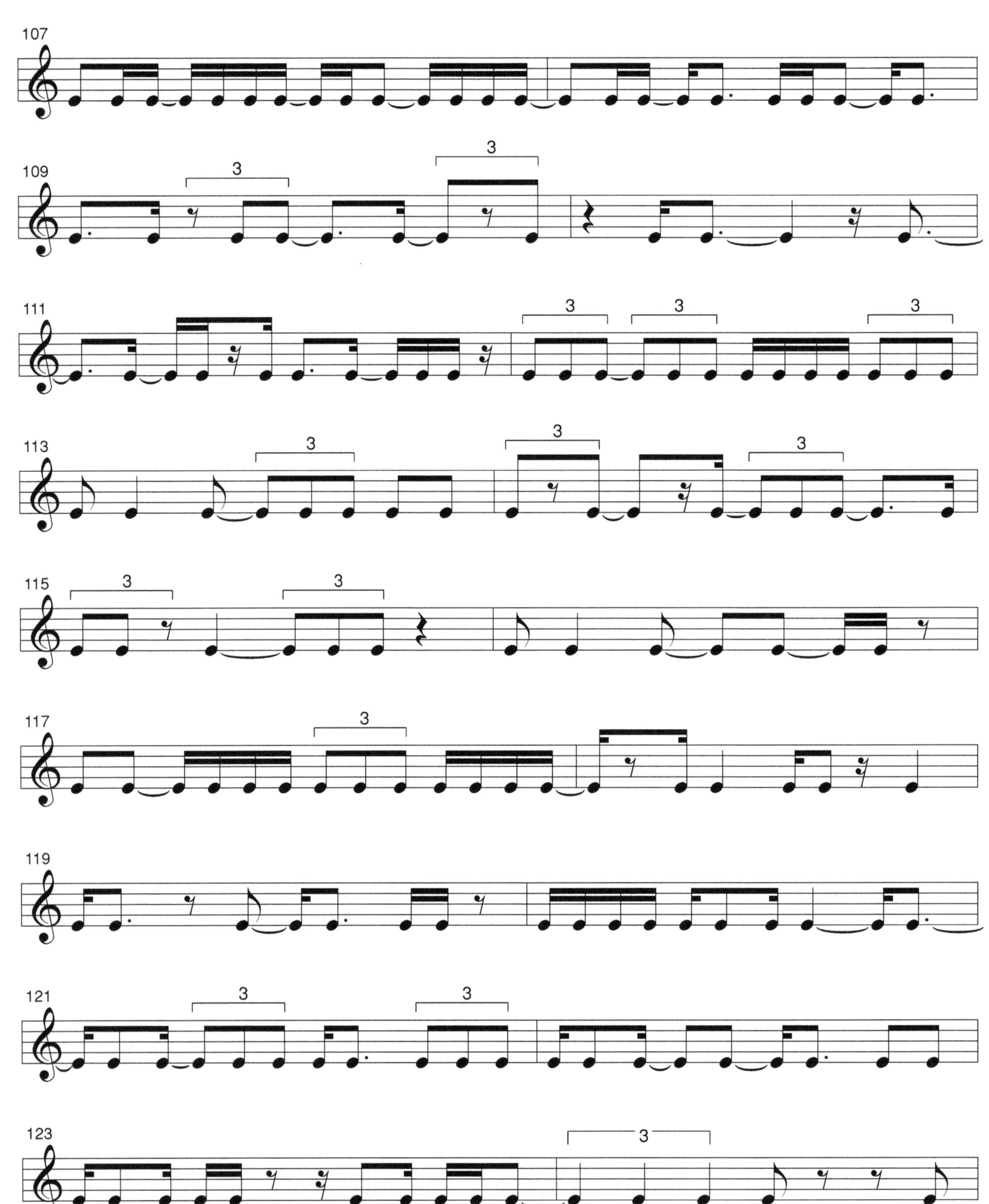
107
109
3
3
111
3
3
3
113
3
3
3
115
3
3
117
3
119
121
3
3
123
3

125
127
129
131
3
3
133
135
137
3
139
141

143
145
147
3
3
149

EXERCISE 9

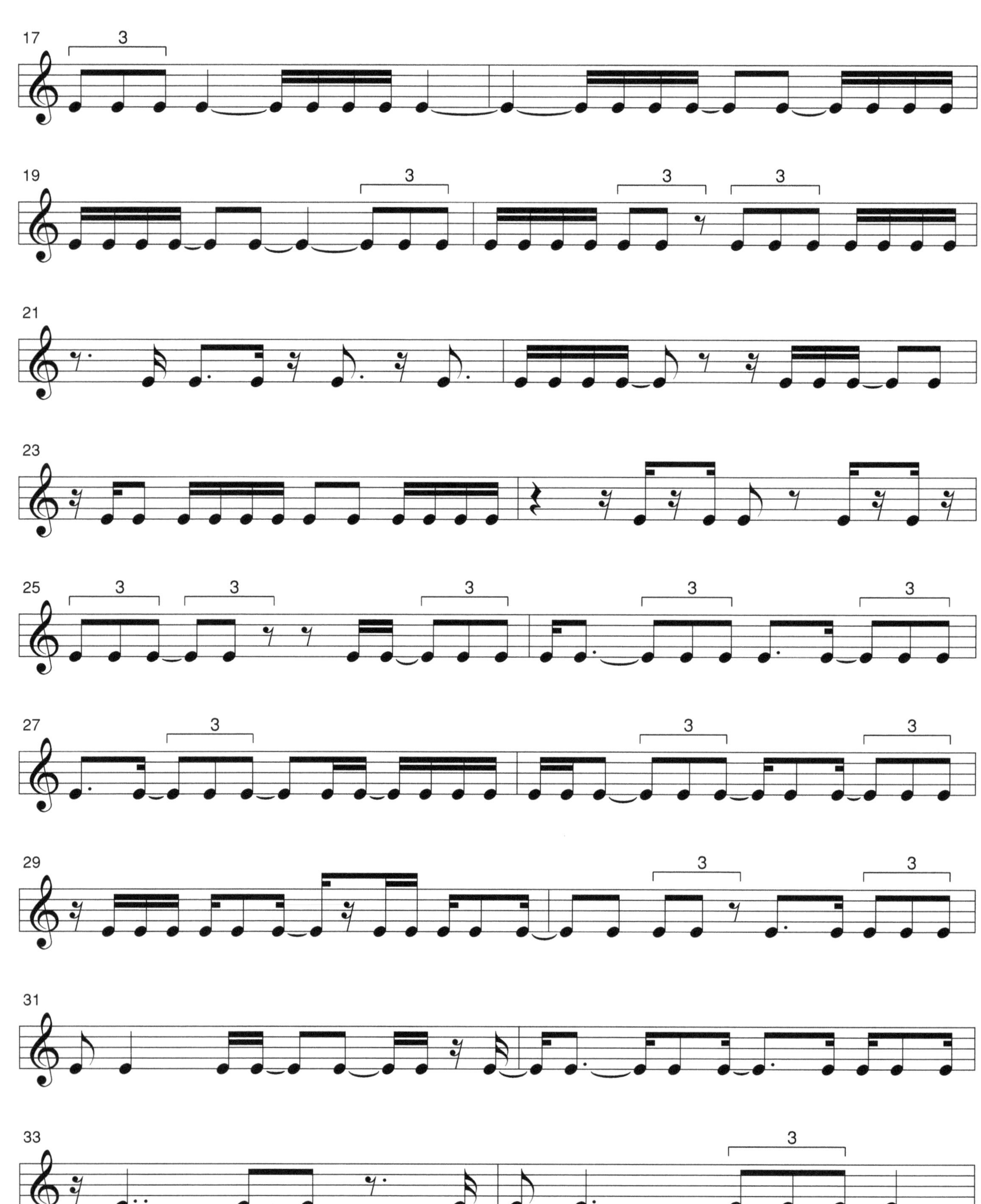
17
3
19
3
3
3
21
23
25
3
3
3
3
3
27
3
3
3
29
3
3
31
33
3

35
3
37
39
41
43
45
3
3
3
47
3
3
49
3
51

53
3
55
57
3
3
59
61
3
3
63
65
3
3
67
69

71
73
3
75
77
3
79
81
83
85
87
3
3

89
91
3
3
93
95
3
3
3
3
3
97
3
3
99
101
3
3
103
105

107
109
111
113
115
3
117
3
3
119
121
123
3
3

125
3
3
3
127
3
3
3
3
129
131
3
3
133
3
3
3
135
3
3
137
3
3
139
141
3

143
3
3
145
147
149
3
3

EXERCISE 10

17
19
21
23
25
27
29
31
33
35

37
39
41
43
45
3
47
49
3
3
3
51
53
3
3
3
55
3
3

57
59
3
3
3
3
3
61
3
3
3
63
3
3
65
3
3
67
69
71
73
3
3
3
75
3

77
79
3
81
83
3
3
85
3
87
89
91
93
95
3
3

97
99
101
103
105
107
109
111
113
115

117
3
119
3
3
121
123
125
3
3
3
3
127
3
129
131
3
133
135
3
3
3

137
139
141
143
145
3
3
147
3
3
149
151
153
3
155

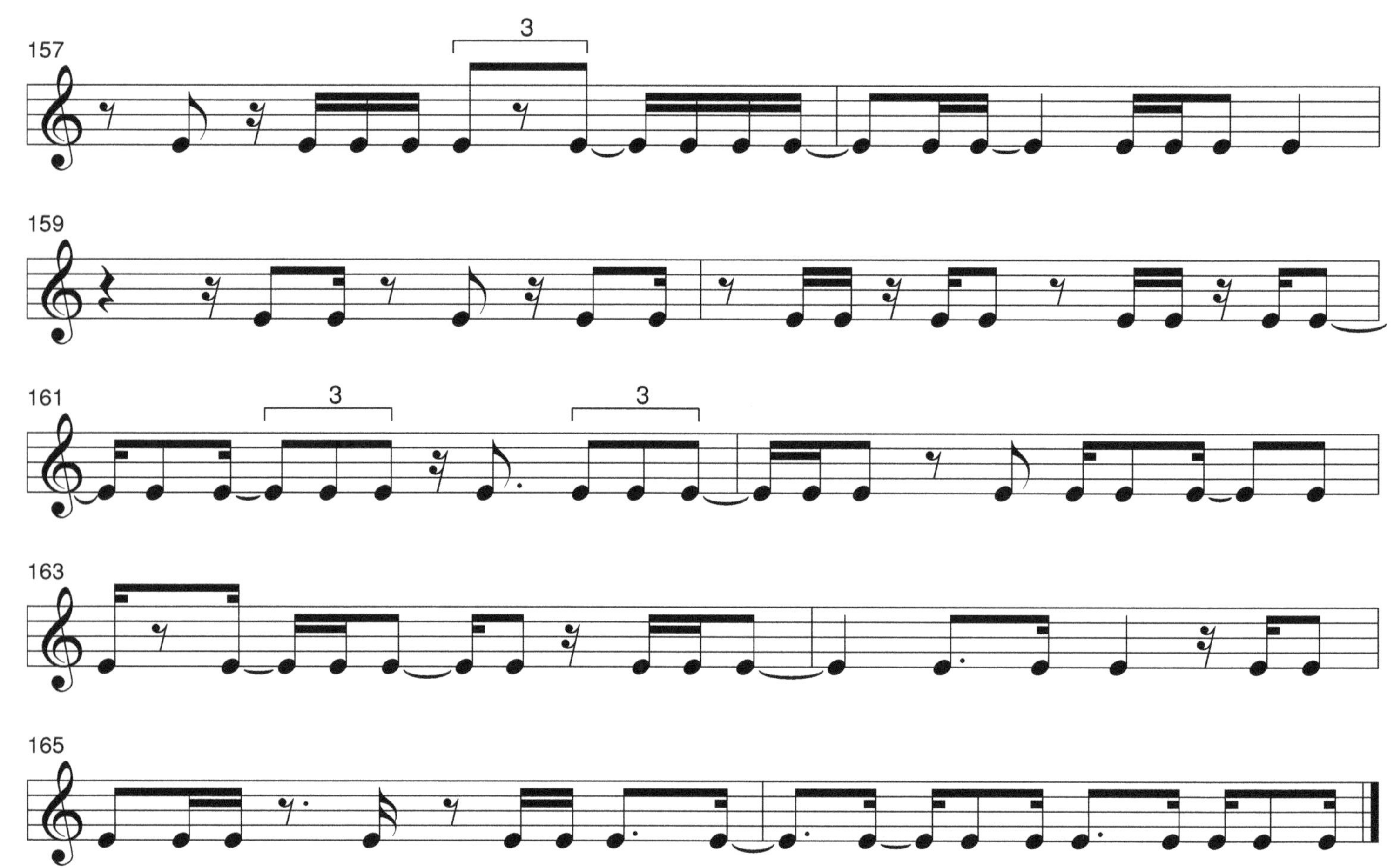
157
3
159
161
3
3
163
165

EXAMPLE 11

17
3
3
19
21
23
25
3
27
29
3
31
33
35

37
3
39
41
43
3
45
3
3
3
47
49
3
3
51
53
55

57
59
61
63
65
67
69
71
73
75

77
3
79
3
3
3
81
83
85
3
87
3
3
3
89
3
91
3
93
3
95
3

97
99
101
103
105
107
109
111
113
115

117
119
121
3
123
3
3
125
3
127
129
3
3
3
3
3
131
3
133
3
135

137
3
3
139
3
3
141
3
143
145
147
3
149
151
3
153
3
155
3
3

157
3
3
159
161
163
3
3
3
165

EXERCISE 12

17
3
3
19
3
21
3
23
25
3
3
27
29
31
33
35
3
3
3

37
39
41
3
3
43
3
45
3
47
49
3
3
51
3
3
53
55
3
3

57
59
61
63
65
67
69
71
73
75
3

77
79
81
83
85
87
89
91
93
95

97
99
3
3
101
3
103
105
3
107
3
109
3
3
3
3
111
3
3
113
115

117
119
121
123
125
127
129
131
133
135

137
3
3
139
3
3
3
3
141
143
145
147
3
3
3
3
149
151
153
3
3
155

157
159
161
3
3
163
3
3

Books Available From
Muse Eek Publishing Company

The Bruce Arnold series of instruction books for guitar are the result of 20 years of teaching. Mr. Arnold, who teaches at New York University and Princeton University has listened to the questions and problems of his students, and written forty books addressing the needs of the beginning to advanced student. Written in a direct, friendly and practical manner, each book is structured in such as way as to enable a student to understand, retain and apply musical information. In short, these books teach.

1st Steps for a Beginning Guitarist
Spiral Bound ISBN 1890944-90-4 Perfect Bound ISBN 1890944-93-9

"1st Steps for a Beginning Guitarist" is a comprehensive method for guitar students who have no prior musical training. Whether you are playing acoustic, electric or twelve-string guitar, this book will give you the information you need, and trouble shoot the various pitfalls that can hinder the self-taught musician. Includes pictures, videos and audio in the form of midifiles and mp3's.

Chord Workbook for Guitar Volume 1 (2nd edition)
Spiral Bound ISBN 0-9648632-1-9 Perfect Bound ISBN 1890944-50-5

A consistent seller, this book addresses the needs of the beginning through intermediate student. The beginning student will learn chords on the guitar, and a section is also included to help learn the basics of music theory. Progressions are provided to help the student apply these chords to common sequences. The more advanced student will find the reharmonization section to be an invaluable resource of harmonic choices. Information is given through musical notation as well as tablature.

Chord Workbook for Guitar Volume 2 (2nd edition)
Spiral Bound ISBN 0-9648632-3-5 Perfect Bound ISBN 1890944-51-3

This book is the Rosetta Stone of pop/jazz chords, and is geared to the intermediate to advanced student. These are the chords that any serious student bent on a musical career must know. Unlike other books which simply give examples of isolated chords, this unique book provides a comprehensive series of progressions and chord combinations which are immediately applicable to both composition and performance.

Music Theory Workbook for Guitar Series

The world's most popular instrument, the guitar, is not taught in our public schools. In addition, it is one of the hardest on which to learn the basics of music. As a result, it is frequently difficult for the serious guitarist to get a firm foundation in theory.

Theory Workbook for Guitar Volume 1
Spiral Bound ISBN 0-9648632-4-3 Perfect Bound ISBN 1890944-52-1

This book provides real hands-on application of intervals and chords. A theory section written in concise and easy to understand language prepares the student for all exercises. Worksheets are given that quiz a student about intervals and chord construction using staff notation and guitar tablature. Answers are supplied in the back of the book enabling a student to work without a teacher.

Theory Workbook for Guitar Volume 2
Spiral Bound ISBN 0-9648632-5-1 Perfect Bound ISBN 1890944-53-X

This book provides real hands-on application for 22 different scale types. A theory section written in concise and easy to understand language prepares the student for all exercises. Worksheets are given that quiz a student about scale construction using staff notation and guitar tablature. Answers are supplied in the back of the book enabling a student to work without a teacher. Audio files are also available on the muse-eek.com website to facilitate practice and improvisation with all the scales presented.

Rhythm Book Series

These books are a breakthrough in music instruction, using the internet as a teaching tool! Audio files of all the exercises are easily downloaded from the internet.

Rhythm Primer
Spiral Bound ISBN 0-890944-03-3 Perfect Bound ISBN 1890944-59-9

This 61 page book concentrates on all basic rhythms using four rhythmic levels. All examples use one pitch, allowing the student to focus completely on time and rhythm. All exercises can be downloaded from the internet to facilitate learning. See http://www.muse-eek.com for details

Rhythms Volume 1
Spiral Bound ISBN 0-9648632-7-8 Perfect Bound ISBN 1890944-55-6

This 120 page book concentrates on eighth note rhythms and is a thesaurus of rhythmic patterns. All examples use one pitch, allowing the student to focus completely on time and rhythm. All exercises can be downloaded from the internet to facilitate learning. See http://www.muse-eek.com for details.

Rhythms Volume 2
Spiral Bound ISBN 0-9648632-8-6 Perfect Bound ISBN 1890944-56-4

This volume concentrates on sixteenth note rhythms, and is a 108 page thesaurus of rhythmic patterns. All examples use one pitch, allowing the student to focus completely on time and rhythm. All exercises can be downloaded from the internet to facilitate learning. See http://www.muse-eek.com for details.

Rhythms Volume 3
Spiral Bound ISBN 0-890944-04-1 Perfect Bound ISBN 1890944-57-2

This volume concentrates on thirty second note rhythms, and is a 102 page thesaurus of rhythmic patterns. All examples use one pitch, allowing the student to focus completely on time and rhythm. All exercises can be downloaded from the internet to facilitate learning. See http://www.muse-eek.com for details.

Odd Meters Volume 1
Spiral Bound ISBN 0-9648632-9-4 Perfect Bound ISBN 1890944-58-0

This book applies both eighth and sixteenth note rhythms to odd meter combinations. All examples use one pitch, allowing the student to focus completely on time and rhythm. Exercises can be downloaded from the internet to facilitate learning. This 100 page book is an essential sight reading tool.
See http://www.muse-eek.com for details.

Contemporary Rhythms Volume 1

Spiral Bound ISBN 1-890944-27-0   Perfect Bound ISBN 1890944-84-X

This volume concentrates on eight note rhythms and is a thesaurus of rhythmic patterns. Each exercise uses one pitch which allows the student to focus completely on time and rhythm. Exercises use modern innovations common to twentieth century notation, thereby familiarizing the student with the most sophisticated systems likely to be encountered in the course of a musical career. All exercises can be downloaded from the internet to facilitate learning. See http://www.muse-eek.com for details.

Contemporary Rhythms Volume 2

Spiral Bound ISBN 1-890944-28-9   Perfect Bound ISBN 1890944-85-8

This volume concentrates on sixteenth note rhythms and is a thesaurus of rhythmic patterns. Each exercise uses one pitch which allows the student to focus completely on time and rhythm. Exercise use modern innovations common to twentieth century notation, thereby familiarizing the student with the most sophisticated systems likely to be encountered in the course of a musical career. All exercises can be downloaded from the internet to facilitate learning. See http://www.muse-eek.com for details.

Independence Volume 1

Spiral Bound ISBN 1-890944-00-9   Perfect Bound ISBN 1890944-83-1

This 51 page book is designed for pianists, stick and touchstyle guitarists, percussionists and anyone who wishes to develop the rhythmic independence of their hands. This volume concentrates on quarter, eighth and sixteenth note rhythms and is a thesaurus of rhythmic patterns. The exercises in this book gradually incorporate more and more complex rhythmic patterns making it an excellent tool for both the beginning and the advanced student.

Other Guitar Study Aids

Right Hand Technique for Guitar Volume 1

Spiral Bound ISBN 0-9648632-6-X   Perfect Bound ISBN 1890944-54-8

Here's a breakthrough in music instruction, using the internet as a teaching tool! This book gives a concise method for developing right hand technique on the guitar, one of the most overlooked and under-addressed aspects of learning the instrument. The simplest, most basic movements are used to build fatigue-free technique. Exercises can be downloaded from the internet to facilitate learning. See http://www.muse-eek.com for details.

Single String Studies Volume One

Spiral Bound ISBN 1-890944-01-7   Perfect Bound ISBN 1890944-62-9

This book is an excellent learning tool for both the beginner who has no experience reading music on the guitar, and the advanced student looking to improve their ledger line reading and general knowledge of each string of the guitar. Each exercise concentrates the students attention on one string at a time. This allows a familiarity to form between the written pitch and where it can be found on the guitar along with improving one's "feel" for jumping linearly across the fretboard. Exercises can be downloaded from the internet to facilitate learning. See http://www.muse-eek.com for details.

Single String Studies Volume Two
Spiral Bound ISBN 1-890944-05-X   Perfect Bound ISBN 1890944-64-5

This book is a continuation of Volume One, but using non-diatonic notes. Volume Two helps the intermediate and advanced student improve their ledger line reading and general knowledge of each string of the guitar. Each exercise concentrates the students attention on one string at a time. This allows a familiarity to form between the written pitch and where it can be found on the guitar along with improving one's "feel" for jumping linearly across the fretboard. Exercises can be downloaded from the internet to facilitate learning. See http://www.muse-eek.com for details.

Single String Studies Volume One (Bass Clef)
Spiral Bound ISBN 1-890944-02-5   Perfect Bound ISBN 1890944-63-7

This book is an excellent learning tool for both the beginner who has no experience reading music on the bass guitar, and the advanced student looking to improve their ledger line reading and general knowledge of each string of the bass. Each exercise concentrates a students attention of one string at a time. This allows a familiarity to form between the written pitch and where it can be found on the bass along with improving one's "feel" for jumping linearly across the fretboard. Exercises can be downloaded from the internet to facilitate learning. See http://www.muse-eek.com for details.

Single String Studies Volume Two (Bass Clef)
Spiral Bound ISBN 1-890944-06-8   Perfect Bound ISBN 1890944-65-3

This book is a continuation of Volume One, but using non-diatonic notes. Volume Two helps the intermediate and advanced student improve their ledger line reading and general knowledge of each string of the bass. Each exercise concentrates the students attention on one string at a time. This allows a familiarity to form between the written pitch and where it can be found on the bass along with improving one's "feel" for jumping linearly across the fretboard. Exercises can be downloaded from the internet to facilitate learning. See http://www.muse-eek.com for details.

Guitar Clinic
Spiral Bound ISBN 1-890944-45-9   Perfect Bound ISBN 1890944-86-6

Guitar Clinic" contains techniques and exercises Mr. Arnold uses in the clinics and workshops he teaches around the U.S.. Much of the material in this book is culled from Mr. Arnold's educational series, over thirty books in all. The student wishing to expand on his or her studies will find suggestions within the text as to which of Mr. Arnold's books will best serve their specific needs. Topics covered include: how to read music, sight reading, reading rhythms, music theory, chord and scale construction, modal sequencing, approach notes, reharmonization, bass and chord comping, and hexatonic scales.

Sight Singing and Ear Training Series

The world is full of ear training and sight reading books, so why do we need more? This sight singing and ear training series uses a different method of teaching relative pitch sight singing and ear training. The success of this method has been remarkable. Along with a new method of ear training these books also use CDs and the internet as a teaching tool! Audio files of all the exercises are easily downloaded from the internet at www.muse-eek.com By combining interactive audio files with a new approach to ear training a student's progress is limited only by their willingness to practice!

A Fanatic's Guide to Ear Training and Sight Singing

Spiral Bound ISBN 1-890944-19-X   Perfect Bound ISBN 1890944-75-0

This book and CD present a method for developing good pitch recognition through sight singing. This method differs from the myriad of other sight singing books in that it develops the ability to identify and name all twelve pitches within a key center. Through this method a student gains the ability to identify sound based on it's relationship to a key and not the relationship of one note to another (i.e. interval training as commonly taught in many texts). All note groupings from one to six notes are presented giving the student a thesaurus of basic note combinations which develops sight singing and note recognition to a level unattainable before this Guide's existence.

Key Note Recognition

Spiral Bound ISBN 1-890944-30-0   Perfect Bound ISBN 1890944-77-7

This book and CD present a method for developing the ability to recognize the function of any note against a key. This method is a must for anyone who wishes to sound one note on an instrument or voice and instantly know what key a song is in. Through this method a student gains the ability to identify a sound based on its relationship to a key and not the relationship of one note to another (i.e. interval training as commonly taught in many texts). Key Center Recognition is a definite requirement before proceeding to two note ear training.

LINES Volume One: Sight Reading and Sight Singing Exercises

Spiral Bound ISBN 1-890944-09-2   Perfect Bound ISBN 1890944-76-9

This book can be used for many applications. It is an excellent source for easy half note melodies that a beginner can use to learn how to read music or for sight singing slightly chromatic lines. An intermediate or advanced student will find exercises for multi-voice reading. These exercises can also be used for multi-voice ear training. The book has the added benefit in that all exercises can be heard by downloading the audio files for each example. See http://www.muse-eek.com for details.

Ear Training ONE NOTE: Beginning Level

Spiral Bound ISBN 1-890944-12-2   Perfect Bound ISBN 1890944-66-1

This is a new method for developing instantaneous recognition of pitches within a key. This contextual-based ear training differs from interval based training by instilling a sense of key relationship; that is, a note is identified by it's characteristic sound within a key, and not by its distance from another note. This method has been used with great success and is now finally available on CD. There are three levels available depending on the student's ability. This beginning level is recommended for students who have little or no music training. A Complete Method book containing the Ear Training One Note Beginning, Intermediate and Advanced levels along with three accompanying CDs is also available for those students wishing to have a complete set of books and CDs under one cover.

Ear Training ONE NOTE: Intermediate Level

Spiral Bound ISBN 1-890944-13-0   Perfect Bound ISBN 1890944-67-X

This is a new method for developing instantaneous recognition of pitches within a key. This contextual-based ear training differs from interval based training by instilling a sense of key relationship; that is, a note is identified by it's characteristic sound within a key, and not by its distance from another note. This method has been used with great success and is now finally available on CD. There are three levels available depending on the student's ability. This intermediate level is recommended for students who have had some music training but still find their skills need more development. A Complete Method book containing the Ear Training One Note Beginning, Intermediate and Advanced levels along with three accompanying CDs is also available for those students wishing to have a complete set of books and CDs under one cover.

Ear Training ONE NOTE: Advanced Level

Spiral Bound ISBN 1-890944-14-9   Perfect Bound ISBN 1890944-68-8

This is a new method for developing instantaneous recognition of pitches within a key. This contextual-based ear training differs from interval based training by instilling a sense of key relationship; that is, a note is identified by it's characteristic sound within a key, and not by its distance from another note. This method has been used with great success and is now finally available on CD. There are three levels available depending on the student's ability. This advanced level is recommended for advanced music students or those who have worked with the intermediate level and now wish to perfect their skills. A Complete Method book containing the Ear Training One Note Beginning, Intermediate and Advanced levels along with three accompanying CDs is also available for those students wishing to have a complete set of books and CDs under one cover.

Ear Training ONE NOTE: Complete Method

Spiral Bound ISBN 1-890944-47-5   Perfect Bound ISBN 1890944-48-3

This is a new method for developing instantaneous recognition of pitches within a key. This contextual-based ear training differs from interval based training by instilling a sense of key relationship; that is, a note is identified by it's characteristic sound within a key, and not by its distance from another note. This Complete Method book contains the Ear Training One Note Beginning, Intermediate and Advanced levels along with three accompanying CDsand is available for those students who wish to have a complete set of books and CDs under one cover.

Ear Training TWO NOTE: Beginning Level Volume One

Spiral Bound ISBN 1-890944-31-9   Perfect Bound ISBN 1890944-69-6

This Book and Audio CD continues the method of developing relative pitch ear training as set forth in the "Ear Training, One Note" series. There are six volumes in the beginning level series. Through practice, the student eventually gains the ability to recognize the key and the names of any two notes played simultaneously. Volume One concentrates on 5ths. Prerequisite: a strong grasp of the One Note method.

Ear Training TWO NOTE: Beginning Level Volume Two
Spiral Bound ISBN 1-890944-32-7 Perfect Bound ISBN 1890944-70-X

This Book and Audio CD continues the method of developing relative pitch ear training as set forth in the "Ear Training, One Note" series. There are six volumes in the beginning level series. Through practice, the student eventually gains the ability to recognize the key and the names of any two notes played simultaneously. Volume Two concentrates on 3rds. Prerequisite: a strong grasp of the One Note method.

Ear Training TWO NOTE: Beginning Level Volume Three
Spiral Bound ISBN 1-890944-33-5 Perfect Bound ISBN 1890944-71-8

This Book and Audio CD continues the method of developing relative pitch ear training as set forth in the "Ear Training, One Note" series. There are six volumes in the beginning level series. Through practice, the student eventually gains the ability to recognize the key and the names of any two notes played simultaneously. Volume Three concentrates on 6ths. Prerequisite: a strong grasp of the One Note method.

Ear Training TWO NOTE: Beginning Level Volume Four
Spiral Bound ISBN 1-890944-34-3 Perfect Bound ISBN 1890944-72-6

This Book and Audio CD continues the method of developing relative pitch ear training as set forth in the "Ear Training, One Note" series. There are six volumes in the beginning level series. Through practice, the student eventually gains the ability to recognize the key and the names of any two notes played simultaneously. Volume Four concentrates on 4ths. Prerequisite: a strong grasp of the One Note method.

Ear Training TWO NOTE: Beginning Level Volume Five
Spiral Bound ISBN 1-890944-35-1 Perfect Bound ISBN 1890944-73-4

This Book and Audio CD continues the method of developing relative pitch ear training as set forth in the "Ear Training, One Note" series. There are six volumes in the beginning level series. Through practice, the student eventually gains the ability to recognize the key and the names of any two notes played simultaneously. Volume Five concentrates on 2nds. Prerequisite: a strong grasp of the One Note method.

Ear Training TWO NOTE: Beginning Level Volume Six
Spiral Bound ISBN 1-890944-36-X Perfect Bound ISBN 1890944-74-2

This Book and Audio CD continues the method of developing relative pitch ear training as set forth in the "Ear Training, One Note" series. There are six volumes in the beginning level series. Through practice, the student eventually gains the ability to recognize the key and the names of any two notes played simultaneously. Volume Six concentrates on 7ths. Prerequisite: a strong grasp of the One Note method.

Comping Styles Series

This series is built on the progressions found in Chord Workbook Volume One. Each book covers a specific style of music and presents exercises to help a guitarist, bassist or drummer master that style. Audio CDs are also available so a student can play along with each example and really get "into the groove."

Comping Styles for the Guitar Volume Two FUNK
Spiral Bound ISBN 1-890944-07-6   Perfect Bound ISBN 1890944-60-2

This volume teaches a student how to play guitar or piano in a funk style. 36 Progressions are presented: 12 keys of a Major and Minor Blues plus 12 keys of Rhythm Changes A different groove is presented for each exercise giving the student a wide range of funk rhythms to master. An Audio CD is also included so a student can play along with each example and really get "into the groove." The audio CD contains "trio" versions of each exercise with Guitar, Bass and Drums.

Comping Styles for the Bass Volume Two FUNK
Spiral Bound ISBN 1-890944-08-4   Perfect Bound ISBN 1890944-61-0

This volume teaches a student how to play bass in a funk style. 36 Progressions are presented: 12 keys of a Major and Minor Blues plus 12 keys of Rhythm Changes A different groove is presented for each exercise giving the student a wide range of funk rhythms to master. An Audio CD is also included so a student can play along with each example and really get "into the groove." The audio CD contains "trio" versions of each exercise with Guitar, Bass and Drums.

Bass Lines: Learning and Understanding the Jazz-Blues Bass Line
Spiral Bound ISBN 1-890944-94-7   Perfect Bound ISBN 1890944-95-5

This book covers the basics of bass line construction. A theoretical guide to building bass lines is presented along with 36 chord progressions utilizing the twelve keys of a Major and Minor Blues, plus twelve keys of Rhythm Changes. A reharmonization section is also provided which demonstrates how to reharmonize a chord progression on the spot.

Time Series

The Doing Time series presents a method for contacting, developing and relying on your internal time sense: This series is an excellent source for any musician who is serious about developing strong internal sense of time. This is particularly useful in any kind of music where the rhythms and time signatures may be very complex or free, and there is no conductor.

THE BIG METRONOME

Spiral Bound ISBN 1-890944-37-8   Perfect Bound ISBN 1890944-82-3

The Big Metronome is designed to help you develop a better internal sense of time. This is accomplished by requiring you to "feel time" rather than having you rely on the steady click of a metronome. The idea is to slowly wean yourself away from an external device and rely on your internal/natural sense of time. The exercises presented work in conjunction with the three CDs that accompany this book. CD 1 presents the first 13 settings from a traditional metronome 40-66; the second CD contains metronome markings 69-116, and the third CD contains metronome markings 120-208. The first CD gives you a 2 bar count off and a click every measure, the second CD gives you a 2 bar count off and a click every 2 measures, the 3rd CD gives you a 2 bar count off and a click every 4 measures. By presenting all common metronome markings a student can use these 3 CDs as a replacement for a traditional metronome.

Doing Time with the Blues Volume One:

Spiral Bound ISBN 1-890944-17-3   Perfect Bound ISBN 1890944-78-5

The book and CD presents a method for gaining an internal sense of time thereby eliminating dependence on a metronome. The book presents the basic concept for developing good time and also includes exercises that can be practiced with the CD. The CD provides eight 8 minute tracks at different tempos in which the time is delineated every 2 bars, and with an extra hit every 12 bars to outline the blues form. The student may then use the exercises presented in the book to gain control of their execution or improvise to gain control of their ideas using this bare minimum of time delineation.

Doing Time with the Blues Volume Two:

Spiral Bound ISBN 1-890944-18-1   Perfect Bound ISBN 1890944-79-3

This is the 2nd volume of a four volume series which presents a method for developing a musician's internal sense of time, thereby eliminating dependence on a metronome. This 2nd volume presents different exercises which further the development of this time sense. This 2nd volume begins to test even a professional level player's ability. The CD provides eight 8 minute tracks at different tempos in which the time is delineated every 4 bars with an extra hit every 12 bars to outline the blues form. New exercises are also included that can be practiced with the CD. This series is an excellent source for any musician who is serious about developing an internal sense of time.

Doing Time with 32 bars Volume One:
Spiral Bound ISBN 1-890944-22-X   Perfect Bound ISBN 1890944-80-7

The book and CD presents a method for gaining an internal sense of time thereby eliminating dependence on a metronome. The book presents the basic concept for developing good time and also includes exercises that can be practiced with the CD. The CD provides eight 8 minute tracks at different tempos in which the time is delineated every 2 bars, with an extra hit every 32 to outline the 32 bar form. The student may then use the exercises presented in the book to gain control of their execution or improvise to gain control of their ideas using this bare minimum of time delineation.

Doing Time with 32 bars Volume Two:
Spiral Bound ISBN 1-890944-23-8   Perfect Bound ISBN 1890944-81-5

This is the 2nd volume of a four volume series which presents a method for developing a musician's internal sense of time, thereby eliminating dependence on a metronome.. This 2nd volume presents different exercises which further the development of this time sense. This 2nd volume begins to test even a professional level player's ability. The CD provides eight 8 minute tracks at different tempos in which the time is delineated every 4 bars with an extra hit every 32 bars to outline the 32 bar form. New exercises are also included that can be practiced with the CD. This series is an excellent source for any musician who is serious about developing an internal sense of time.

Other Workbooks

Music Theory Workbook for All Instruments, Volume 1: Interval and Chord Construction
Spiral Bound ISBN 1890944-92-0   Perfect Bound ISBN 1890944-46-7

This book provides real hands-on application of intervals and chords. A theory section written in concise and easy to understand language prepares the student for all exercises. Worksheets are given that quiz a student about intervals and chord construction using staff notation. Answers are supplied in the back of the book enabling a student to work without a teacher.

E-Books

The Bruce Arnold series of instructional E-books is for the student who wishes to target specific areas of study that are of particular interest. Many of these books are excerpted from other larger texts. The excerpted source is listed for each book. These books are available on-line at www.muse-eek.com as well as at many e-tailers throughout the internet. These books can also be purchased in the traditional book binding format. (See the ISBN number for proper format)

Chord Velocity: Volume One, Learning to switch between chords quickly

E-book ISBN 1-890944-88-2 Traditional Book Binding ISBN 1-890944-97-1

The first hurdle a beginning guitarist encounters is difficulty in switching between chords quickly enough to make a chord progression sound like music. This book provides exercises that help a student gradually increase the speed with which they change chords. Special free audio files are also available on the muse-eek.com website to make practice more productive and fun. With a few weeks, remarkable improvement by can be achieved using this method. This book is excerpted from "1st Steps for a Beginning Guitarist Volume One."

Guitar Technique: Volume One, Learning the basics to fast, clean, accurate and fluid performance skills.

E-book ISBN 1-890944-91-2 Traditional Book Binding ISBN 1-890944-99-8

This book is for both the beginning guitarist or the more experienced guitarist who wishes to improve their technique. All aspects of the physical act of playing the guitar are covered, from how to hold a guitar to the specific way each hand is involved in the playing process. Pictures and videos are provided to help clarify each technique. These pictures and videos are either contained in the book or can be downloaded at www.muse-eek.com This book is excerpted from "1st Steps for a Beginning Guitarist Volume One."

Accompaniment: Volume One, Learning to Play Bass and Chords Simultaneously

E-book ISBN 1-890944-87-4 Traditional Book Binding ISBN 1-890944-96-3

The techniques found within this book are an excellent resource for creating and understanding how to play bass and chords simultaneously in a jazz or blues style. Special attention is paid to understanding how this technique is created, thereby enabling the student to recreate this style with other pieces of music. This book is excerpted from the book "Guitar Clinic."

Beginning Rhythm Studies: Volume One, Learning the basics of reading rhythm and playing in time.

E-book ISBN 1-890944-89-0 Traditional Book Binding 1-890944-98-X

This book covers the basics for anyone wishing to understand or improve their rhythmic abilities. Simple language is used to show the student how to read and play rhythm. Exercises are presented which can accelerate the learning process. Audio examples in the form of midifiles are available on the muse-eek.com website to facilitate learning the correct rhythm in time. This book is excerpted from the book "Rhythm Primer."

www.ingramcontent.com/pod-product-compliance
Ingram Content Group UK Ltd.
Pitfield, Milton Keynes, MK11 3LW, UK
UKHW061830190726
13855UKWH00005B/1742

9 781890 944568